HOUSE
and
GARDEN

Books by John Engels

The Homer Mitchell Place (University of Pittsburgh Press, 1968)

Signals From the Safety Coffin (University of Pittsburgh Press, 1975)

Blood Mountain (University of Pittsburgh Press, 1977)

Vivaldi in Early Fall (University of Georgia Press, 1981)

Weather-Fear: New & Selected Poems (University of Georgia Press, 1983)

The Seasons in Vermont (Tamarack, 1983)

Cardinals in the Ice Age (Graywolf Press, 1987)*

Walking to Cootehill: New & Selected Poems (Middlebury: University Press of New England, 1993)

Big Water (Lyons & Burford, 1995)

Sinking Creek (Lyons Books, 1998)

National Poetry Series Selection

HOUSE
and
GARDEN

 JOHN ENGELS

University of Notre Dame Press
Notre Dame, Indiana

Manufactured in the United States of America

*Acknowledgments**
Columbia, "Eve in the July Garden," "Adam after the Ice Storm"*
Georgia Review, "Adam and the Voice of the Wind"*
Kenyon Review, "Adam Imagines Moving"*
Notre Dame Review, "Adam in the Late Dusk of Some Summer Night,"* "Adam
    and the Heron"*
Sewanee Review, "Eve Sleepless"
Shenandoah, "Eve Complaining of the Heat"*
Southern Review, "Adam and the Raccoon"*

"The Guardian of the Lakes at Notre Dame," "Eve Awakening," and "Adam Sign-
ing" appeared in different forms and with different titles in *Walking to Cootehill:
New & Selected Poems 1958–1992* (Middlebury: University Press of New England,
1992) pp. 53–57. "Adam in the Third Week of November" appeared in *Sinking
Creek* in a different form and under another title.

*These poems were published under different titles.

Library of Congress Cataloging-in-Publication Data
Engels, John.
House and garden / John Engels.
p. cm.
ISBN 0-268-03056-1 — ISBN 0-268-03057-x (pbk.)
1. Adam (Biblical figure)—Poetry.   2. Eve (Biblical figure)—Poetry.
3. Married people—Poetry.   4. Housekeeping—Poetry.
5. Vermont—Poetry.   I. Title.
PS3555.N42 H65   2001
811'.54—dc21

                                                    2001003554

For my grandchildren

Henry and Molly and Eliot

in whom the word roots, leafs, and blossoms

Contents

The Guardian of the Lakes at Notre Dame   1

Adam Looking Down   4

Adam Remembers Moving   5

Eve among the Willows   7

Adam Considers His Death   9

Adam among the Silences   11

Eve Measuring the Distances   13

Adam in Late March   14

Eve in April   16

Adam and the Heron   17

Eve among the Trees at Night   19

Adam in the Late Dusk of a Summer Night   21

Adam Seeing Double   22

Adam in the Garden at Night   23

Adam Picking Herbs   25

Eve Complaining of the Heat   28

Adam in Fall   29

Eve Sees Storm Light on the Mountain   30

Eve Thinking Back   31

Adam Suffers Regrets in October   32

Adam and the Voice of the Wind   34

Eve Sleepless   35

Adam and the Wind at Night   36

Eve at the Edge of Winter   37

Adam at Noon   39

Adam Opening the Clam   41

Eve and the Ash Tree   42

Adam and the Raccoon   44

Eve and the Great Circle   45

Adam Transplanting Perennials   47

Adam Fears Fire   49

Eve in the Garden at Night   50

Adam at Moonrise   52

Eve Dancing among Moon Shadows   53

Eve and the Comet   54

Adam Pruning Lilacs   55

Eve Overlooking the Garden   58

Adam among the Perennials   60

Adam Considering the Rugs   62

Adam at the Bathroom Mirror   63

Eve at the Looking Glass   64

Eve Considers the Possibility of Resurrection   65

Eve Considers the Possibility of Pardon   68

Eve Walking at Dawn   70

Adam in November   71

The Neighborhood Prepares Itself for Melancholy   73

Adam after the Ice Storm   74

Eve at First Light   76

Adam and the Cardinal at the Window   78

Eve Overlooking the Lake   79

Adam in the Third Week of November   81

Adam in the Graveyard   82

Poem in Late February   83

Adam and Eve and the Orders   84

Adam Thinking Back   86

Adam Signing   88

Adam Awakening   89

Eve in the Garden at First Light   90

Adam Recounting the Seasons   92

HOUSE
and
GARDEN

The Guardian of the Lakes
at Notre Dame

I cannot any longer bring to mind
the name of the ancient, hated Brother
who patrolled the lakes at Notre Dame
and ran the kids off, waving an old gun

from the far shore, shouting in a voice
that from one hundred yards away
seemed dangerous as a sword blade.
Retired to guard the lakes, the old man did;

and for him to wake up was to most powerfully insist
that turtles be troubled merely to feed,
herons to fly, snakes to dream of toads.
Himself the caring center of all careless natural grace,

at last he died. The lakes were fished.
There is perhaps something to say
in favor of old men who raise
the guardian arm and voice against

the hunting children—who, but lately come
to Paradise, pursue the precedent beast
unto its dumb destruction, and persist.
And surely the sky came more and more to seem

like the dark-enclosing vault
of the dead box turtle's shell. Perhaps
he thought to cry against the children
was like love, love

being often in rebuke of innocence.
In the event, they plundered the far shore,
and he waved his gun, and shouted out at them
go home! go home! *in stern fierce order*

that they might be made to see
how in the end the bellowing angel had raised
fist and sword, and thus they would come to be
forfeit of name in the memories of men.

Adam Looking Down

From the hilltop at the edge of the pine grove
I look down onto the blooming orchards.
I watch the slow emergence

of spring. I feel
obligation of retrieval.
The air carries with it

the taste of mushrooms, apples,
the smell of sour muds. Far below
the orchards blossom, the season

is gathering. I look down
on the resumptive body of the world,
on whatever I am obliged

to make of it to see or touch,
by which necessity
it will bear names, and be.

Adam Remembers Moving

One gets used to everything.
It's painful to recognize
the skill we have at it.

What we really desire
is to be alive in somebody's
eyes, we line up to be

remembered. In the bedroom
when the bed is taken out, there
is the floor showing

the honey-brown of the old pine boards
in the shape of the bed, painted around,
surrounded by a glossy field, a garden plot

of green-going-to-black,
one of the spaces to be
dispensed with, disposed of utterly,

and helpless against being
returned to. To walk
through the dark doors

and find we are no longer in
has to be watched out for.
There are rules for this kind of thing,

severe penalties once
we exceed the boundaries
of the general unhappiness. Whatever

is lost or out of place
of the place we lived in—I don't mean
the ordinary landscapes

of the house, lightfall
in a room, or the peculiar
echoes of closets, earth smell

of basements, water stains shaded
and contoured to the shapes
of a woman's face, a map,

or nothing but a water stain—I don't mean
these things, they
are recoverable, they insist

on their availability. I mean everything
closed off from view, and one day
released to the dumb lament. Make it

so that I can say it plainly, if not simply,
let these things go down with me.
Keep me faithful to loss.

Eve among the Willows

Among the yellow branches
a feathering of wind, dusts
of sun through the little holes
in the green shade. Our voices,

quiet enough from the very first,
have long ago been swallowed up
in the leafy whisperings of this place.
And where we cannot

and will never again see them,
the great flowers of the garden,
alive to the memory of light,
must still reach and blossom

and breathe their showy breaths. As for us,
oh, our hearts
beat so inexpertly when we looked
at one another! What he heard and saw

I was never able to tell, so that I
would never become
of like mind with him. Now I believe
we've always lived

as we were meant to live,
here in the middle of a world
that burgeons coldly around us,
in the yellow dust of a dry sun

and this green mottling of narrow leaves. Here
is where we've made our home.
I think our hearts
may well have outlived our voices.

These big willows seem borne down,
though in fact they strive equally
to sun as to earth. We walked
under trees like these, heavy

on the world, in such a gravity
not even silence escaped us.

Adam Considers His Death

Please let it be
the work of an instant!
Do not require us to wake slowly
under a burden of earth

smothered in a web of roots. I wonder—
this morning in which I lie
awake, breathing freely, speaking
to you from the shadow of these willows

a lively sky sparking through
the moving leaves—as I will wonder
in that morning to come,
which I so fear: *how*

will we be different? Forgive us, allow us
this one peace, in which
if we must leave at all,
the warm earth will stir

and fold softly back
and we'll fly from our graves
into a fine brightness,
our bodies new and shining,

the last grains of the planet
sifting through our fingers,
the petals of our hearts
trembling to life,

beginning to move again, let it be
that we will be no less at peace
than ever . . . but no more! It must have been
you loved us after all,

for having called on us to die,
you left us trapped in yearning.
Oh that was a gift! We would not otherwise
have reveled so in hope.

Adam among the Silences

I looked to myself for the names
among those first silences,
thinking of them
as I thought of my hands

where they newly moved before me,
clasped and unclasped themselves,
stroked the sides of my face, shielded
my eyes from the sun

and every weather—I
had not commanded them,
they knew by themselves they had to come
to terms with my face, my eyes,

each other, they had
obligations—but always
they went about their business
without sound, wordless, foreknowing

they had to perish . . .
whereas beyond what I could see
the sky thinned
into utter colorlessness

though from somewhere
came light enough that through my hands
before my eyes I saw
thin blood-colored translucencies

and heard a heart beat
brittle as the first crinkling skin
of the first ice. But my tongue
did not hurry to help me out.

I will never know what it was feeling then.
My tongue seemed willing to wait
for a long time, it was at least
always faithful to the silences—

I am willing to confess that,
alone among much from which I turn away.
As for my hands, they stroke
the sides of my face, shield

my eyes from the sun
and every weather,
every turn of the blood—and still
I do not command them

but have come too late and far too late
to this business
of putting names. What I heard and saw
I can never tell—but what I came to

finally were the silences.
What I entrusted myself to
was not then clear to me, nor now,
but what it came to

were the silences. For all
the labyrinthine babble, straight lines
on the page, the world's gone on
in its great stillnesses without me.

Eve Measuring the Distances

We should have understood. Distance
measured itself from where
we lay or walked or slept.
Birds sang to be heard.

Light found us
so that it might be seen.
We were given to see
the clear orders of Paradise,

each morning the earth
came about us, an ocean
of flowers and leaves, then
fields, waves, seas of color

that rushed on and away to break
in the distance on the icy mountains
where it must have been
nothing could live.

Adam in Late March

The season's a buffeting of desolation, nights
like breath stopping, days
the bore of the wilderness flooding
these dry lawns. And onto the lawn where I am standing,

by virtue of an afternoon's high wind, the elm,
of its green self almost wholly shed, scatters
most of its dying crown, and I snatch up and shatter
huge branches of deadwood against

the rotting bole, make piles of slash, set fires
all over the yard and garden, so that in the growthless afternoon
of this day in this late March, my hands
fiery with shock, everything around me ablaze as if

the muddy fires of the Torment have broken through,
it breaks through in me
how the season is neither generous nor kind,
and how we suffer the belief that we

will never be alone, that the still presence
of the beloved is more sure than that the absence
has been spoken, and long ago, and endures. In a rage
that lasts all afternoon, legs akimbo, body bent and braced,

I swing with all my strength at the beetle-ridden bark,
smash and splinter every branch I can lift, heave it
onto the fires, or stab with the jagged butt
into the soft lawn until it strikes and stops on ice, stab

and stab at the muddy earth in plain assault
on what does not love or has abandoned me, the season
straining to brighten itself, myself
straining to believe there is in fact everywhere about me

a loosening earth, a greening of lawns through the scurfs
of all the grassy years that have passed into the violence
of termination, this last ice-edge of season, the season's
most bitter concurrence in the stern orders of loss.

Eve in April

April: which is to say
by my measure some small
equivocal truth about how everything

takes place at the wrong time. The black
locusts seem dead, the maples
have come half-alive and wait.

In this garden, in all the gardens
of the neighborhood, the spring muds
steam, and from time to time

something like the sun
takes place. For the moment
all the doors stand open,

the house airing, readying itself,
and by evening the spring frogs
will be chirping and roaring away

from the ditches, and one
which all winter had been hiding there
will sing out from the cellar.

Adam and the Heron

Gathering marsh marigolds,
on the lookout for sundews, orchids,
pitcher plants, I come
on this flat clot of muddy feathers

in the shape of a heron, head
caught back in the slow contraction,
and then a hundred yards out
a great blue heron takes flight

just as I begin plucking the long hackles
from the smelly flesh
to rib my spey flies,
and so of course I have to stop

what I'm doing, and watch
his huge awkwardness
utterly transform itself, long legs
streaming out behind, big wings

after the first few embarrassing flaps
strong and steady, neck
curved back a little, the marsh
still echoing some with the gross

croaking of his fear, but nothing
to pay attention to: he was flying,
and watching him I kept on trying to pull
dead feathers from the dead bird,

both of us earthbound and flightless,
both in our own ways gone heavy, tugged
at the beautiful gray-blueness of feathers
that even rooted in that week-old

stinking vulgarity
of movelessness, resisted, seemed
somehow to pull back.

Eve among the Trees at Night

Maples overhang the deck.
We live fully among trees.
It's different up here,
not at all the same as wandering in a grove,

leaning up against a rough trunk,
stumbling on a root—
no, the true life of trees is above us,
especially, I think, when the sun glints

through the interstices of moving leaves
and dapples earth and body
so that one comes to seem
almost the other. During the day

the trees mediate between light and us,
but at night up here among the leaves,
the pines sighing but ready to roar, the aspens
fluttering, the maples

ashuffle with rustlings,
the stars breaking a little
through the leaves,
below us in the lightless garden—

which all day drowned
in the shadows of trees, and every night
lies bone-still in the planet's shadow—
below us in the still garden,

sunflowers and roses,
primroses closed tight
on daylight, the light
of yards and houses

and of the flowers themselves
folding in on the planet's heart,
the day disappearing before
our astonished eyes—

and then the great cyclonic ebbing of light
that froths and currents
about the roots of the big trees—
at such times

the trees are given to speaking
most clearly
and we most given
the grace to hear.

Adam in the Late Dusk of a Summer Night

In the late dusk of some summer night
when the garden has grown
to its fullnesses of blossoming and fragrance,

and she is standing at the window, half-
asleep, eyes half-closed, the stars
sharpening to brittle points, the night

on the other hand delicate
in its embraces, dawn
already impatient for its turn, I'll come,

because I'll know she is expecting me,
and arrive with my eyes fixed on her thoughts,
the night dense in my nostrils

as in hers, the stars
grown needle-keen. Because the place
is nothing, because it's unimportant,

we'll leave it behind; but as for time,
I suppose that must travel with us.

Adam Seeing Double

A cloud of early morning light,
fog of gold and silver: the fields
of the world blur. To look into this light

must be what it is to stare up
from a great deepness
through the blind sea to where the sea

concludes itself and gives over
to that instant of sea and air
neither water nor breathable, a fiery membrane

of gold and silver. Over the garden the sun
multiplies, the clouds
explode into something

like huge peonies, luminous
concentricities of leaves, bright rays
of petals, everything outlined

in the radiance of its shape . . .
and through this density of light
what might be a face

looks back, though
it ripples and changes, so
forms and vaporously unforms,

that what it might have shaped
itself into of love,
anger, or even of hatred, is unclear.

Adam in the Garden at Night

Let's face it, our bodies were not
much inclined to one another's.
All that time everything
was preparing itself. All those nights

the house lay open,
the fragrance of *nicotiana*
flooded the rooms—the gardens
were preparing themselves

for full bloom, and without knowing it
I was getting ready for tonight,
to stand here framed in a window
of this many-windowed room

trying to see down into the garden,
trying to see how it handles itself at night,
for instance, if starlight or moonlight is worth
anything to it, or if there might be flowers

burdened by the moon, or that turn their faces
to the moon, or some others
compelled to faintest
star or planet light. One truth, though,

about the garden at night: it's full
of silence. All
that silence! It's enough to stock
a hundred, a thousand poems!

Believe me, I'm happy for it, silence and I
have always been close. But in the house,
standing at the window, the garden dealing
with night in its own many ways,

I'm compelled to regard myself
in the dull mirrors of memory,
and while the world's
gone small, memory's

hugely blooming with pity, rage,
hatred, nothing there, really,
about love, love is beside
the point, it's not

the point at all, I've missed
the point, it's not
what we've been talking about.
And, very slowly, the sky

goes pious with sunlight,
and the gardens tremble, preparing
to wake to all our patent brightnesses.

Adam Picking Herbs

One after the other
I pinch a needle of rosemary,
a leaf of basil, thyme, of golden

oregano, one blossom
from the apple mint, a fistful
of tarragon, and scrub my hands

with dirt between each small harvesting—
all this leading to the dill
which beyond all other smells

the garden has to offer
opens itself to me—
but I take them all in,

eyes closed, hold them in—
trusting they'll take on shapes—
though I'd be helpless to say

the shape of a smell, however skillfully
at the drop of a hat
I dredge up small talk

about what's hidden
in objects—but I'm stuck with this—
dirt on my wrists and palms,

and under my nails, green stains
on my fingers, sweet coalescences
of bruised herbs—yet

there's much to regret
about the gardens I cobble together
in what I conceive to be

the image of the first.
I came here not understanding
I was from a place, but then

saw mountains to either side, no access
to horizons—and knew, straightaway
the terms of loneliness, that first winter,

snow to the windowsills,
thin flurries of icy light
scattering themselves

over the yards and gardens.
And I'm still here, in the same light,
and the mountains still encroach,

mornings deeply shadowed with them,
their shadows coming over the garden
from the east, evenings from the west,

snow, rain, sun, fog, smoke
occupying what's between.
It's another spring, like all

the others, the buds on the maples sticky,
catkins lengthening and dangling
from the willows, cherries, peaches,

apples ready to bloom. Whatever
I may think, I don't want
to return to where

I came from, though I can't deny
it calls to me. There are mountains
between us. I live

at this coupling
of shadows, in a dusk
like sleep. It's just

that I came from *there,*
from the enormous fields
in my memory always

laid out before me
in the colors of ripening. Somehow
I can't recall snow, though

I must be wrong, it must
have snowed. But it doesn't matter,
I can't unassign the name. The truth is

here. I stand in a window of this house,
mountainous shadows flowering
in the gardens. *I'm here.*

The incident is closed.

Eve Complaining of the Heat

All night it seemed a giving off of voices
from the garden, an occasional
soft fragrance of joy, malodor

of rage or desolation, often
long silences of the kind
that exist only before

what is about to be spoken
is spoken—then nothing
but the rise and fall of wind

which carried nothing
in it of discourse or cadence,
but was merely wind.

Now, this morning, the flowers
are mute, their leaves droop
with an early heat, and the trees

look to be molting. A rankness of ivy
smothers the roadsides. I expect the gardens
to seethe all day without a word.

Adam in Fall

"*Fall*." That word. Our word.
A triumph, as triumphs go
these days, a little glimmer

in the moving shadows of memory—
Mostly we've lost the talent
for words. But now and then

something breaks through,
from back, far back, just enough
that our hearts leap, the word

forms itself, and for once, for a moment,
the earth comes alive,
and we take it back

into ourselves, and it lodges there,
begs our forgiveness
for what out of no will at all

it's spelled out
of all that's fallen away, of all
that's abandoned, unrecognizable.

Were we in love back then? We'll never know.
Time's silent on the matter. It's just
that now we're here, walking together

alone, under the lowering skies,
in the light of the unspeaking world.

Eve Sees Storm Light on the Mountain

On the mountain this morning
I saw clouds rooted

in gray layers of undershadow
piling, billowing, even roaring up,

and wide blades of sunlight
slicing through, long slivers

of light slanting eastward
from peak to foothills,

striping the mountain
orange, scarlet and yellow,

the mountain—
until at last rain came

and the sun wholly failed—precisely
verging on fire.

Eve Thinking Back

Outside, the dense quiet
of an October rain, a cool rising
of pines on the hill, and the lake

bursting on its reefs, feathering there,
wash of passage, night noise of water
widening shoreward to meet

house lights which have spread
outward in a thin wash
over the lake. I look over the lake,

and think back
through the thick drifts of time
and come upon

this place, this one house,
the one water, beneath it all
 a rising ice. It seems

about to be in the way of a naming.
I turn back into the house, close doors,
lock windows on the cold fires the house

has lent the lake. Tonight
the world is still, though in an instant
anything could change.

Adam Suffers Regrets in October

October evenings, in the face of the last
gatherings of light, more largely, even,
in the face of the last gatherings
of all the sweet bodies of the summers

to which in our uncommon time
the earth has given rise, it's come to seem
more than ever much to ask
that nothing should be asked, that it is necessary

to be without need, that nothing
in the way of anger, bitterness, death or desire
is forgiven, or even unforgiven;
that what one desires of the other

is required to be taken, or gone without.
This is what comes of whatever may have been
in the beginning, by reason of which
each of us might have gone on

to love the other. This
is what comes of it, and it breaks through to me
how the season is neither generous nor kind,
and that we have seemed to affront it,

for having believed we might never die;
that the still presence of the voice within us,
in which we might have spoken to whom
we might have loved, is more certain

than its absence. Meantime
I breathe in these risings of night air.
October lies at the edges of my pillow. October
is the first edge of the fall: that

is its consonance, and this thought
so intervenes to my special sorrow
that therefore is my heart now more than ever
borne in upon by the heavy body

it has been accustomed to sustain.

Adam and the Voice of the Wind

The wind sang about my house. The gardens
sang back. The weathers were difficult. The voice
too was difficult, though it sang back

to the wind, knowing neither
its honor nor its place. Never doubting
its happiness, it sang *me! It's me!* It thought

it knew my name. Forever it chose me,
I never knew its mind. And now this voice insists
it is not nothing to have ceased

being loved. It's trying to find a name
for itself, it's in a hurry, it's trying
to absolve me of my life, it's trying

to tell me if there's to be life,
then life is to be this way.

Eve Sleepless

Downstairs everything
is where it ought to be,
in place, a serenity

of rugs and furniture,
though in the night
the storm door flung itself open

and three times banged hard shut,
and each time the hot night shimmered
and a long dreamlessness

stretched ahead. The cat cried,
water drizzled in the sink.
Outside the weathers gathered,

blood thumped
in my ear.

Adam and the Wind at Night

The door slammed three times in the night
and I started up not really having heard,
but more *felt* the noise,

shuddered some, and as always
in such circumstances,
I was alarmed, as always ready

for invasion. Presently I crept
downstairs, alert to any peculiar
density of shadow, to anything

moving, or seeming about to move,
but everything was as it ought to be,
a stillness of rugs and furniture, only

the storm door flung open
and three times banged hard shut
by sudden gusts of a night wind.

I hooked it shut. Back in bed,
I gave up on sleep, it was early yet,
a long night stretched ahead,

I was discomposed,
it only works one way, one
cannot be alarmed back into sleep.

But my head thudded
with possibility.

Eve at the Edge of Winter

What hierarchy of love and choice
shall have exacted it of us,
that to the shame of all our yearning
the body goes foul on its bones, beyond

its own or any pardon?
The sky already is quivering
with snow, and I think how it was
all summer the leaves of the McIntosh

were green as I have imagined ice
at the hearts of glaciers to be green,
while in July there were times
when, about to sleep, I might have sworn

that by morning the lawns would be stiff with frost,
the calendulas collapsed on their stems,
petals corollas of golden ice;
might equally have sworn

that in August one dawn I awakened
to a blizzard—though it was only
a swarming of white butterflies at a dead mole
in the grass. All summer

and well into the fall we worked
in the old orchard cutting apple wood,
three cords of it split and stacked
and just in time. Now, yet only October,

snow storms at the edges of the lawn.
I close the door,
light up the first fire of the year,
and outside the weathers are gathering.

Adam at Noon

By noon what's left
of the sky has faded
into the neighborhoods,
and the late roses
give off a cold smell.
The first souring

of wet leaves is likewise
cold, and the chill eye
of the October night
crowds up to the windows
and stares in. Furniture

dims in the clouding rooms,
and in October I begin
to move carefully, take cover
in shadows, among the tall grasses
of the season become

especially vigilant,
looking around me, hoping
it is not for me as it is
for the trees, skies, roses.
But already the breath

has begun to sour
in my throat. Duration
draws a circle around me. I live
amidst conspiracies of furniture. Overhead

the sun shows no warmer
than the moon. The door of the sky
swings closed. The leaves
have begun their tiresome fall.

Adam Opening the Clam

Once I stood on a beach, the sea
washing the sand from under
my feet, and held the muddy stone
of a clam, pried with my knife
at the lip, and as the muscle tore
and gave, noticed a stirring

in the shallows, a small eddying
of bottom sand, a flurry
of sand eels, and then a calm
so absolute I was startled, and looked down

into the open shell onto a flesh
which must have just cried out
with a sound beyond my hearing, looked down
onto a pearly flesh more like the sea

than any but the plasms
of my own sperm.

Eve and the Ash Tree

October has always seemed
an error of time—who will not argue
that in Vermont it is

the freshest of seasons, the loveliest,
most to be loved? Yet in one night
the big ash deposits its leaves

in a litter of gold
all over the back half
of the garden, which sight

always startles me, this failure
of the leaves—though I should know
and well enough by now

there is nothing about the ash tree moderate,
gradual or considered, as with
the maple, nor obstinate,

as with the oak. I've learned
to expect that around the middle
of October will occur overnight

this storming of leaves. This year
I see it once more in the way
I've never understood,

as if the given day
were to be the last on which
I might perceive such a thing

as the unlit brilliance
of these ash leaves.
Not for the first time

the sight has reminded me
of something I've been unable
to name, have seen

only dimly and on occasion
during the time of the failure of leaves
when it still seems possible

that winter will not come
and the warm hazes of October will lie
about the open-windowed houses

of the neighborhood; in which
it still seems possible
that on a following night

the leaves might burst up from the grass
like a flushed covey of small
golden birds, and rearrange themselves

on the branches, so that in the morning
I'd find the garden
shaded again, yet a residual

brightness on the flower beds
beneath the reawakened
light-feeding tree.

Adam and the Raccoon

I saw him a little before dawn
in the dense growth of the daylilies
and ferns at the far back of the garden
against the fence, creeping

along the fence, small shadow, stopping,
peering about, casting about, cautious for dog
or cat smell, and I kept too far away
for him to notice, and kept still, and strained

to keep him from getting lost
in the general shadow, to keep
from mistaking
his shadow for something else

not alive, or not alive as he
was alive . . . then heard him
at one of the apples I'd earlier thrown
out there against the fence hoping

just this . . . to have seen him there,
wild shadow near to being lost
in the shadows of the garden,
to have drawn him there, to have known

he would come, to have known
he could not help but come. Oh, that
undeviating determination
to hunger! He will die for it one of these days!

Eve and the Great Circle

The sky is beginning to tremble with rain again—
the puddles from the last storm
merely half-dried—but the gardens
are grateful, the weight of the winter

lifted from them, and they open themselves
to any sky awash with rain or sun,
it doesn't matter to them, their roots
spread and tangle every which way

patternless, in dumb commotion, forcing themselves
up, until abrim with leaves, the gardens tuft, bud, climb
their trellises, in the gardens this endless
dim flowing of green shadow, and then the flowers

return—and standing here
in the middle of all this I catch myself
asking for life—all around me
fleabane sprouting from the asphalt, the phlox

explosions of pink and blue, scarlet and claret,
climbing roses and clematis
shuddering with color, and the whole
bald dome of the sky awash

with rain and sun—it's purely
beautiful, I don't know why,
the flowers having come around again
in their great circling, I should be

so disheartened—maybe
it's too regular, too easy, the mind after all
rejoicing in disunities, most jubilant
in irresolution, and this resurgence of the gardens

is common, too easy, nothing in it
of the desirable silence, nothing
motionless, no hint
of the dead pole,

the leafless core of the world
about which we most naturally
in our steadfast immobility
of change, I mean

our happiness, dance awobble
on the great circle of the ecliptic—all
this ascending and descending of saps and juices,
this huge formality of growth—it's

unnatural, it's not the work
I accomplish alone, or with you,
or with anyone.

Adam Transplanting Perennials

An afternoon of spring light, the trees still waiting for leaves
and there arrives a power of rain, which dwindles
to something almost inexpressible
in the way of rain, a good day

to transplant azalea and rhododendron to fill in
the vacancies of winterkill, as well as the Purple Gem
mowed down by accident last fall. The first spadeful,
the first jab deep into the soil, and there wells up

a wild odor of earth, of severed maple roots,
bruised grass; another and the general air floods
the hole—nothing then but a moldiness
and souring of wet catkins, some faint inkling

of low tide, and even that dissolved
in the morning light…you'd think
from all I've said this must have been like opening
a grave—but I swear to you my youth shot up over me

with that first fragrance in that early morning
spring light like the light of almost-waking, this lightstream
I awakened merely by scooping out a hole, these recollections
all winter buried deep, rooted and stirring in me

like some disconcerting dream, subcorporeal
vegetation of anger, sorrow and regret—not that I slept
to this dream, far from it, only that it shadowed me
backward, its long emberous tail, dwindling fast

from one light to the next to the last incoherent luminosity
of the last hard kernel of fire long
beyond long in repose—but then
the slow outblooming of the fire's seed,

from the planet's fervid center.

Adam Fears Fire

But what is the man, otherwise courageous, to do
who fears fire, who thinks of himself afire
crying out, hair aflame, bones crumbling

to coals, when it is the cold
that rightly should frighten him,
for everywhere he looks, in all the sleets

and rockscapes of the work, everywhere
the fragile spawns of the ice
flower and heave up

his lawns, everywhere
they are springing up
and blazing forth, like trees of fire!

Eve in the Garden at Night

When at last the shadow of our house
dissolved into the gardens
and our eyes were still snowblind, at least a little,

we thought *spring, spring!*
but then the night swept over us
and we no longer could see

with any confidence—except once we thought
the neighbors embraced in their windows
then looked about as if they thought

we might have been on the verge of noticing.
When the night might have been ended
we pretended to silence,

and then it went on.
We felt our hearts beat angrily
one against the other, and all of this

became one thing that given a name
remained nameless.
We thought back to the time

when we had come together from nothing,
the hope of our time,
hearing the dry leaves of the garden

scraping together, that terrible racheting
of green life, and to the west the sky
torn with clouds, and to the east a ragged moon,

moving over the garden.
We thought back, stranded there
in the odd light of moonset, pretending

to silence, then turned
inside to our rooms—not
that we slept, far from it

Adam at Moonrise

Before me lies the dimness of garden
through the sweet soils of which,
at the same time that it probes toward bedrock

with its tender root, the moon pushes up,
and the garden bulges with it, and soon
the moon will burst free in some sort of bizarre

blossoming—a dim circle of light,
widening in a bright ring,
then crumbling away to each side—and there

will be the moon's bright crown,
then the great body of the thing itself
pulling free, the sands and gravels

of the under soils raining away,
until it has torn free and risen
stemmed with a brilliant tendril

of root, risen and swollen,
grown round on itself
as a great peony in its slow way readying

to open itself out, to fill the sky,
burst out, unfold
into a great flowering of light.

Eve Dancing among Moon Shadows

I doubted my eyes, my various shadows
sometimes twined and twisted like roots
thrusting outward from my feet,

then again flung away,
soft, without edges, diffuse from gold to green
to halos of rusty dun, pouring away over

the undulations of lawn, dying
into the ragged edges
of the fall garden.

I doubted my eyes, danced
and postured. The sky
veiled and unveiled itself.

The moon rode high
and took on shapes
I had never imagined. Clouds

overcame it. Each time
it emerged in a contrary light.
But my shadows

refused me, they flew about
ragged and random as clouds.
They were nothing to do with me.

Eve and the Comet

It is not the final moon, or the last
vestige of sun, or the one dim light
of the last street of my concluding dream

that flickers silver-blue-and-yellow
over the exhausted houses,
the shadowed gardens, and I rejoice

for here is the comet, after years of wishing
and of failed light, here is the comet, about time
I knew it having waited this long time,

my eye wandering the skies,
desiring to rejoice, wishing my eyes
to be flung back by its light—motionless

cold dart of fire, great fiery tear,
as if the sun wept fiery tears,
casting the slight shadow I cast

so it seems slung counter-
sunwise, and flares back
into a lightlessness

deeper than sleep.

Adam Pruning Lilacs

Spindly, leggy, sprouting fringes
of suckers, the lilacs have put their flowers
far out of reach, and I prepare
to cut them back for the sake

of next year's blooms—mount the ladder,
reach up pruning shears in one hand, one hand
for myself, and find myself
wobbly among the blooms, the air weighty

with their perfume—and remember a line
from a poem I can't otherwise
remember: *"Oh, he won't be hanged
until it's lilac time!"* the ladder

unsteady, the front legs in a loose
soil sunken in an inch or so. From here
I see the lake, and the mountains,
the woods gone a sweet green,

and I try to make a shape
of the lilac smell—oddly,
no freshness to it, nothing
warm about it, or breathed out, but somehow

an amplification of colors, the slow lavender
of the blossoms, likewise a cerulean
lightness such as you might expect
of a broken sky, this traced through

with infinitesimal threads of scarlet,
vermilion, blue—and, yes, a slight
chill of gray or white to it,
but all in all a powerful

suffusion of lights, intricate
embroidery of scents—it weighs me down,
and as I propose these futilities
the right leg of the ladder abruptly breaks through

the skin of the garden, and I plunge
through the lilac bush, whipped
by branches, shedding similes
all the way, to flat on my face

in the soft seedbed, warm dirt
in my mouth, nose,
eyes—blind with dirt and breathless—
then catch at my breath and sit up—

spitting, choking, clearing
my eyes—and by God here I am again,
back again to the original light,
from wherever it was

that for a second I was shocked to the notion
I'd started to take root, some flash
of a dream of blooming, some lengthening
upward into leaf-bearing branches—

but only for an instant, no
longer—and I have to get up
and back to the breath and eye
that are hard-bent on the cutting back,

that clamp down hard
on that determination,
though for no more
than a second I breathed in

the same air as the lilac,
in its manner of rooting
reached down.

Eve Overlooking the Garden

The garden has ignited.
It's feverish. Even the white clematis
flutters with sun,

and the red lilies and coral bells
burn back at it. Windblown petals
of cardinals flash

across the buttery primroses:
a good year for gardens.
Everything shines.

I write this standing at my window.
I don't go down into the garden.
From here I see everything

at once, all the flowers trapped
in color, in their showy, slow
ignition—petal, pistil, leaf and stamen

separating off. Perhaps
there is a way
out of such fiery

gorgeousness. It must
be wearing. Even at night
when I've gone blind
I hear this splendid confusion

of harmonics, what only can be
the sharp yellowing
of gloriosas, the speckle-

throated oranging
of the Canada lilies.

Adam among the Perennials

These perennials,
unweeded, unthinned,
and left to go wild,
have won out this year,
have strangled everything
that shouldn't be here.

The earth is choked with growth!
Long ago I had foreseen
this bright day, this empty place.
Well, all to the good. Let the houseplants
burst their pots, let them make it
or not. Let the garden grow

and seed and grow and seed,
dry up, collapse under the fall
leaves, let the composts
commence their rich
fever, let the dead leaves
of the geraniums go

unpicked, let pansies seed,
let leaves and petals blow
into the neighbor's yard
and make colorful drifts
at the roots of his fences.
Nor will I prune the grapevine:

but let it tangle and hood the little
wild apple at the end of the porch, let it
climb as high as it likes, and stop
where it likes. I've decided
the gardener's duty
is to wildness. I'm the only one

who knows how to follow the flagstones,
having placed them here
and for fifteen years,
watched them slowly overgrown
by their ravenous borders.

Adam Considering the Rugs

Sometimes you have to exalt
artifice, especially when
it's useful, as with

rugs, laid down to render
our passages inaudible, proposing us
to ourselves as in our process

weightless—sometimes
it's even good to abandon
reason and all reserve, as now I say

the meaning of this house *lies*
in its rugs: outflowering
its gardens, fierier, more verdant

than its gardens, efflorescences
of oranges, yellows,
carmines and scarlets beyond scarlet,

densities of root hues otherwise true
only beneath the surfaces
of gardens, symmetrical

false dazzlements
of gardens, overdone resiliencies
of bloom, but bearing

in outright color, light
and silence our whole
intolerable weight.

Adam at the Bathroom Mirror

This morning I've awakened
and gone into the bathroom
and still speechless with sleep

glimpsed myself
in the bathroom mirror
and stopped to stare . . .

whatever there may be to say
of dream, of language, of necessity
is here, my waking eyes

dead center looking back,
this day as every other waking day
bound to become the same

slow, enormous ceremony
of retrieval. However the need
maintains us, however

your beautiful agile shape
may have sprung from out
of my sheltering bones, I know

this love of matter to have been
the suicide of angels, its recollection
the last giving-over of the dead.

Eve at the Looking Glass

The house lives its life
without us. Sunlight wanders
its green walls, the mirrors

don't recognize us,
they are intent to reflect
the perspectives of room

on diminishing room,
that close on the vanishing point
of our dead silences,

where we conclude—
and then commence to open,
open and reopen, broaden, cascade

against the blind backs of mirrors
into which in passing
we must from time to time

incuriously have peered, our rooms
gone echoing before us
into the conjunct lightlessness.

Eve Considers the Possibility of Resurrection

I do not want to die,
to fall back, to see
the reverse of things, to decompose

to the source, that absolute
fierce bounty of Desire
from which I sprang.

I have never understood
how it can be the seasonal truths
are kept. I know

that spring is the literal, lemony shoot
of sourgrass in the gardens, then redbud, dogwood,
the air stained with scent and color

for yards around, then the blossoms of cherry,
apple, peach, in the pasture
the white, deadly buttons

of the amanita, on the hill
russula like small hemispheres of fire
in the pine duff. I fear such growing

beyond where it might be recalled
to have begun—now all this life has become
a considered dividing on itself,

flaming outward and back from the fat
sugary summer green, then folding back
onto the root, the horned sun

burgeoning inward
onto an utter density of lightlessness from which
the sky is desperate to rebound. I fear

what may be growing outward, ready
to distend and burst
the tender flesh of the planet, I fear

that at the end my mind will keep on,
will not finally sigh
onto the peaceful inmost seed of dream—all this

though I am made to think
that something will rise, all this
though I have felt

that in my body something
that does not appear within its outline, something
deep and materially hid

which does not advance upon the tomb,
itself suffers, thinks, works, and will be torn away
from the body, all this

seems somehow manifest
in the world's entire life, in each
massive rising of day and night, all this

crying out against the mortal fiction,
all this rising and crying out
in the glorious accents of the particular.

Eve Considers the Possibility
of Pardon

In one dream I am made watchful.
In this dream the name we never clearly have heard
is spoken, which name, if we knew

and could speak it, would call back to us
those whom in time we will have come to love
and who will die; would bring them back to us

like us abandoned again
to his terrible consequence,
the silence between us

forever affirmed. And in whatever
might constitute the pardon
would come down in a fragile rain

the whole matter of all
we will ever love, the whole
fiery blade of space, ten billions of suns

suddenly blossoming small and cool
as snowdrops over the opening graves,
the world shimmering with the blue

delicate membrane of the fallen sky,
while above us the forsaken voice calls out
come back come back

as if calling the name
each of us had long forgotten
until that very instant not remembered

as proper to our hearts.

Eve Walking at Dawn

All night the chained dogs barked
in absolute maniacal meter
and never stopped till dawn.

Others in the woods roamed free
chasing deer, belling in long chords,
but at sunrise quieted. In my dawn walk

at the foot of the hill I came on a hollow
where a doe had been hamstrung and brought down
and fed upon, her violet guts

spilled out onto the pine duff,
and when I walked back to the house
and through the garden, the dawn light

fell all wrong,
my shadow leaped stumps and lay askew
on the lawn, lost itself

in a tumult of peonies, because
I had once more been made
to believe in the large, murderous heart

of the night, in the adversary beasts
of the night.

Adam in November

It was a long fall
after a dry summer, in which
the McIntosh bore for the first time.
Now, even in November,

I smell apples, there is some
virtue of breath at work,
something is moving, the names of things
branch up and there are dreams

in which nothing seems strange. I ought
to have trained myself better to waiting
and even better to silence,
but knowing that I cannot with anything

in the way of grace be properly silent,
cannot edify my image before others
or pretend to much of pride and balance, assume
credible lineaments of virtue, consult

with generosity, love or justice, I tend
to speak though lacking clarity,
not knowing the names, not having in need
the language, given to interminable

revision of the text. And this is where
the true anger locates itself,
that I have no ability or hope
that I may speak to the ordinary

with much in the way of truth or generosity.
And it must seem I make my rituals
to be the sole judge of the truth,
instead of what they are, mere sanctimonies

of procedure . . . and so
the names refuse themselves, and always it ends
in so unsatisfactory an obliquity as this.

The Neighborhood Prepares Itself for Melancholy

The garden's an untended
overgrowth of moonflowers, ragweed,
goldenrod, thickets

of witch grass—it's rusting,
it draws back and buries itself
in what's left of its fragrances.

Sometimes at dusk
I walk into the garden,
shuffle through leaves, pull

a weed or two, examine
the fragile stems of the clematis
for signs of rot or weakness,

pick a handful
of the last of the gloriosas
and cosmos, but in the last analysis

none of this matters, the air
is starting to squeeze
the breath from things,

the world's becoming
a mineral landscape,
it's getting away from me.

Adam after the Ice Storm

The cedars lie uprooted
in the exuberant snow.
But I am unsentimental

about trees, I find it not difficult
to imagine this insult
means nothing to them. Soon enough

will arrive some formal
quickening, then what?
After all what can they know

about what they've become?
Or, for that matter, what
they've been—fine exhalations

swelling into a summer night, blind
windings of roots into the perennial beds,
dispassionate buddings

and unfurlings and spring
never more an observance
than winter? I fail to see

how I cannot be right in this, I think
it's as much for them to slow
into their green chill

as when something
warms in them, begins
to crowd up in them—though

if they are other
than I've made them out to be,
they might from the first

have shared with me
in this ardent confusion.

Eve at First Light

The gardens blur
in this cloud of early light,
the sun multiplies, clouds

like huge peonies explode
into luminous concentricities
of petals, bright rays

of leaves, everything
outlined in radiances
of its own shape.

And through this density
of light, faces
look back, so formed

and variously unformed
that what they might
have shaped themselves into

of love, anger, hatred,
seems unclear. Around me
the house of remembrance

goes still. I stand in my window
overlooking the garden,
it's midnight, and the moon

is creeping in and out
of clouds. I'm near
to dying here,

in this house
where the mirrors speak
only among themselves.

Adam and the Cardinal at the Window

The cardinal battering
his reflection in the window glass
falls dazed to the porch floor.

I tap the window,
but he just lies there, one wing
outspread. He's disheveled, hurt,

maybe dead, seen this way
less red than when
from the edge of my eye I catch him across the yard

flirting from twig to twig of the lilac
or in his long swoop
from fence to feeder. Suddenly

he twitches himself up
and into the air,
and the whole yard,

garden and all, for the instant
ignites, rises from its shadows—
everything notices, it's forever

in us, this hunger
for rush of color, this strong notion
of the blood.

Eve Overlooking the Lake

Outside is the dense quiet of an October rain,
a cool rising of pines on the hill
and the lake bursting on its reefs
feathering there, wash of some passage,

night noise of water widening shoreward
meeting our house lights which spread
back into the lake in a thin wash
and diffusion of fire, and halfway

absorb themselves. What
will come of all this? I look back
through the thick drifts of time
and it seems always to have been gathering

and regathering to this: the one tree,
the one water, beneath it all a rising ice,
the world a fragrance of snow and apples—it seems
all about to be in the way of a naming, except

that what might be spoken outright
in such a place would be in the instant
unspoken. How everything goes still! How the roots
which do not speak grope at the ankle and coil

about the wrist, how the sky, clouds, grass
are preparing to lash themselves
into a million furies, this rain
of matter upon sense so deeply

flooding it that therefore
are the names not made or spoken,
not of any being at the poise of limit
and ready to spring back

onto the original impulse, nor
of any which may have hurled themselves
beyond limit, have gone flailing lightward
as the body, named or not,

for balance must. The lake
distantly whispers. I back away,
into the house, close doors and windows
on the night, on the world out there,

on all the cold blossomings of recognition.

Adam in the Third Week
of November

Snow driving in from the mountains
through full strong sunlight, first snow
of this summery fall still abloom

with cosmos, geraniums, snapdragons
—though the maples
were never fooled, and clattered

bonily night upon night
from the south winds
that smelled to them

like snow. But the snow
held off, though earlier by far
the butternut saw it coming,

and gave up, and started dropping
slippery, unsweepable leaves
all over the driveways and decks—

this in the middle of September
when it wasn't yet clear the weathers
would turn against us,

though of course we ought to have known,
and we did know—though meanwhile
the late flowering astonished us to hope.

—in memory of Joanne Rathgeb

Adam in the Graveyard

How cold it is,
that white sun smoking overhead,
powerful contours of snow

braiding, dividing
around the stones,
sheeting and rumpling as if

something were struggling
to break through.
In this place

memory's no salvation,
there's no cause to wake
or trouble us, in this place love

has dwindled to fatigue
like winter gardens
discarded to this

whirl of dirt,
to these heaviest
of days, to this most durable

of our inclinations.

Poem in Late February

Almost six o'clock, and standing at the end of the drive,
snow shoulder-high on either side
where I heaped it Thursday after the big storm,
I look to the west at a pale lemony sky

just draining away. The days seem
to have strengthened a little.
The light must have been changing
for some days now, but tonight's

the first I've found myself required to notice.
Once it was summer that seemed endless . . .
these days it's the winter, streets of blind windows
leaking pale light. Tonight

I've found myself moved
to a kind of excitement . . .
this dusk may be the end
or a beginning to light, though most probably

just another lingering. It's hard to say
what ought to be made of it.

Adam and Eve and the Orders

In this house
everything is where it ought to be.
The mirrors reflect
a perfect order. We cannot say

the same for what goes on
outside the doors and windows,
wilderness of up-
and-down, slantwise, crosswise,

to-and-from—earth-
eating roots gone
every which way purposeless,
rain, great jumbles of snow,

a cardinal dropping from the cedar
into the spreading of white alyssum—
all the processional put up against
the tranquilities of alignment

at which we've worked: stillness
of knives, spoons, forks
in their drawers,
the calm reaches of carpets,

flat clasp of wallpapers,
and the forceless diagonals
of banisters, even
the unbreathing

stillness of the bouquets
of orange calendulas
in their shaggy symmetries arranged
at the precise centers

of tables. And here we are
standing here, looking on, trembling
with something more we knew,

for which we can invent no theory.

Adam Thinking Back

Here is the dry bed of the river,
and on both sides the tumble of rocks
of the old abutments. Now I walk across
dry shod. And here is the road we followed

as it formed, unrolling itself before us
to lead us . . . where? Neither of us knew
but hoped the other did. We never asked
but each secretly followed the other

as if the other led. Oh, it was another world
that sprang up to each side, trees and flowers,
meadows, rivers. Out there in the farthest distance
loom the mountains that on that day

stirred on the horizon, shifted, upthrust,
then arranged themselves
like clouds, then gave themselves
shape. We never looked behind us. Behind us

the wind exploded like laughter. Ahead was nothing,
if silence is nothing. And to each side
the world kept pace, rooting, blooming,
twisting in the new wind. When we came

to where we are, it was as if
we had always known this place. And here
our hearts came to rest in the great mercy
(though how slowly

I reentered that knowledge!) that I could still
make names, name and in turn be named
as what I entitled changed before
my eyes, so on and on, so that

forever therefore these habitable silences
by the awkward act of my regard flash and blaze
into these so gorgeous variegations! We've lost
the kingdom, but borne away

this greatest of its treasures. So here
in the dry streambed I name
love and *bravery, honor, joy,*
I call out *orange* and *maple tree,*

and when I sleep dream *night,* and waking
whisper, *daylight, day, morning,* think ahead
to that moment when I'll turn to her,
to where she lies asleep,

under the blazing trees beside the dry stream,
the mountains clouding the horizon,
the new word at my lips.

Adam Signing

There in the cool birdlit realms,
my breath drawn out into the sky
which more than myself
had come to wish to breathe, I stood

at the verge of the cliff, far short
of where the impulse to go on
had much lessened; and I stared
down on the Garden's silences

not seeing her, who, in that instant
risen from the light of the yellow
seedling grasses, looked up at me
and could not catch my eye or call out,

somehow signal me, finding herself
to be still faint and tremulous of voice,
the soft flesh of her hands
still taking place; and saw me make

suddenly, without warning, into the milky air,
the difficult signs for *flight,* for
danger, as well as the simpler one
for *love,* not thinking to be seen

or answered, and therefore
gesturing so swift, so gorgeously complex
into the calyx of the sky
that she—looking into the rushed dance

of my hands—in that first
most urgent measure of these silences
could not well follow me.

Adam Awakening

When at last I awakened, she lay
beside me, and reaching out
I touched the warm ridge of her spine,

whereupon the end, the ineloquent function,
began to demonstrate itself,
the silences rising, the frightening stars

overhead, the Great Bear
riding the horizon. Already I knew,
and with that first touch

thought to tell her
it is finished, knowing fully
the lie, knowing

if there was to be silence
it would be measurable,
nor would the need

lessen. *For now,* I thought,
*I touch you with my hands
that are hands. Perhaps later*

*the dust will not forget
what it has loved.*

Eve in the Garden at First Light

I visit the garden in the early morning
before anything is fully awake, the white peonies
too heavy for their stems droop
with dew, and the scarlet poppies

have just begun to open. I trail
a heavy shadow. It's done. Everything is named
that I could name, that I saw
to name. I'm not a fool, much

was beyond me. Too much
was beyond me, much reserved, and now
it's becoming hard to breathe, hard
as at the very first when I required

instruction, those first
gasping breaths and I knew
how easily I might drown in that sweet air,
by virtue of that sweet air,

those first tentative
inspirations on which I hawked and choked—
and then by God it grew easier and evened
and sight cleared and there before me, there they lay

before me, the great meadows and mountains of the world,
the morning rising, and the waters
bursting and flooding up from the deepest centers
of the earth, gathering, currenting, rushing down

to pool in the low voids which filled and overflowed
as I stood still close to breathless watching, all the while
light exploding upward from beyond what I had not yet known
to name as light, whereby I saw, I saw, and saw . . .

Now from beyond the pines at the far edge of the garden
crows call, take fright, flare up in hard black shapes
against the sky, wheel, funnel back, then resettle
into the trees and the business of their voices.

Under the branches, in the green shadows of pines,
the golden duff of pine needles softly
thickens and the morning that enters the grove to drift
among the scaling boles seems the remains of light,

a further morning, a sea of light with no opposing shore.

Adam Recounting the Seasons

Spring evenings near the house
sitting together among
the fiddleheads, trillium, mayapple,
at the foot of the hill, the peepers

whistling and groaning
from the coppery bog,
we would repeat it all,
the whole story, from the beginning.

It was our passion
to have forgotten nothing.
The evenings would go shadowy
with owls and whippoorwills,

and of course we tried to sleep
but our thoughts multiplied
and rounded on themselves,
and we were abandoned to their treachery.

This was in the spring.
In the fall at times we felt otherwise.
In the fall we might well have been
of some more proper order, we called each other

by each other's names, there might well have been
something more between us, and between us
and the clamorous leaves
and the yellowing grass, and the emptying blossoms

of the gardens. In the flowerless winters,
watching the sad gestures
of the falling snow, we considered
what we had become, that we shared

the false brightness snow gave off at night.
In the strong light of winter days
there grew a blueness in the ice
that later would spend itself, give itself up,

to the clear, imperative skies
of earliest summer. In summer
breathing the blind light of the blind sun
we were most capable. By then

everything had rearranged itself.
We tended to blame no one,
not even ourselves, for the warm silences
in which we sometimes thought

we heard our names spoken aloud
from among the arrogant blossomings
of the woods—though not
as if we had been spoken to,

but as if the names were being tested
for the sake of the tongue,
their truth—and we'd fall silent,
we'd sit stock-still, listening. Such evenings

were sadnesses. Such evenings
we were never quite sure
what to do with ourselves, fearful
to sleep, the voice of our dreams advancing on us,

whispering our names, the woods around us,
fruitful with shadow, dark crimsons
and violets of apples and plums.